A PORTRAIT OF THE SEVERN

A Portrait of the Severn

Photographing the River
from the Mountains to the Sea

Chris Morris

TANNER'S YARD PRESS

First published 2006 by Tanners Yard Press

Tanners Yard Press Church Road Longhope GL17 0LA
www.tannersyardpress.co.uk

Designed by Paul Manning
Printed and bound by Gutenberg Press Limited, Malta

British Library Cataloguing in Publication Data
A catalogue record for this book is available from the British Library.

ISBN (2006) 09542096-5-6
(2007) 978-0-9542096-5-0

FRONTISPIECE
The Wrekin, from Cressage Bridge

TITLE PAGE IMAGE
Sheep at Caersws

CONTENTS

FOREWORD

The Severn, at 220 miles, is Britain's longest river. It follows a rather perverse course: rising in central Wales, and flowing north-east, before bending like the handle of a shepherd's crook to make its way south, finally emptying into the Bristol Channel. Geologists and pre-historians have theories that this was not always so. They postulate that the Severn, rather than having to break through the hills of Wenlock Edge, flowed further north and joined the Dee. Even stranger to our modern sense of geography is that it went further across the country and joined the Trent.

A more certain historical perspective begins with the Romans. They named the river Sabrina, after a water goddess, and exploited it as a trade route. It remained Britain's premier highway until the Industrial Revolution, which both embraced and then partially eclipsed it. The original Ironbridge, at the time of building a wonder of industrial possibility, spanned the Severn just downstream of the furnaces of Coalbrookdale: canal development supplemented river trade before usurping its traffic. At the end of the seventeenth century, a time when many never left their own village, the communities thriving along the Severn were socially connected in a way unusual in that pre-road-transport age.

I wanted to photograph this great river in a meaningful way, reflecting its history and culture while still acknowledging the twenty-first century. I didn't want pretty riverscapes for their own sake, or feel that my purpose would be served by dwelling on the architecture of the towns through which the Severn passes. On the other hand, I did not want my interest in industrial history to dictate the agenda and overtake the visual possibilities of the river. I hope I have achieved a balance, where the pictures can be appreciated for their own sake as well as being justified by their connections.

I hope also that I have captured the ever-changing mood of the river as it alternates between pastoral tranquillity and its role as commercial servant. I have included something of the canals which have a direct interface with the river and its development. I believe in giving my pages a human face, and I have included anyone I met on my journeys who I felt had a contribution to make.

Please excuse me for not providing a map: almost all the places mentioned feature in a road atlas and more serious students of the river would surely use the Ordnance Survey 1:50,000 series. The sequence of photographs is almost entirely with the flow of the river, at least until Gloucester, where, to suit the subjects, it varies a little – rather like the river itself from then on, with its shifting sandbanks and tidal reverses.

This book is not a comprehensive catalogue of all aspects of the Severn; omissions range from commercial water extraction to leisure activities like dinghy sailing and regattas. Nevertheless it embraces a sufficient variety of river life for me to claim it as my personal portrait. While my print presentation is largely conventional photo quality, digital methods have enabled me to keep close control over such technicalities as perspective, colour quality and tonal values. Most of the photographs were taken in the spring and early summer of 2006; three images first appeared in one of my previous books *(see page 128)*.

Facing page: *Newnham, dawn over the oxbow bend*

1 OUT OF THE MOUNTAINS: PLYNLIMON TO WELSHPOOL

The Severn's source is high on the eastern side of the ridge of Plynlimon, some fifteen miles east of Aberystyth in central Wales. Plynlimon is nearly two and a half thousand feet high, but the summit ridge is more like the Derbyshire Pennines than rocky Snowdonia, with black 'hags' of peat standing up from ill-defined marshy slopes. Britain's longest river rises in one of these swampy areas, with water visible higher or lower on the mountain depending on the season.

The story really starts a thousand feet lower in a Forestry Commission car park. I had walked to the source some thirty years ago and remembered a thick forest laced with fallen trees and strength-sapping bilberry; it was impossible to follow the river up the mountain. The only real choice was to climb up the Forestry roads to the treeline and then strike out across the wet mountainside, looking for the source in one of many boggy hollows.

This time I readied myself for that wet final section by wearing wellington boots. What I didn't know was that the Forestry Commission have laid a superb hard path right up through the woods; as a bonus, cleared sections of the forest give a fine sense of space to the fledgling river which the route directly follows. On the open mountain a complete line of slabs, dropped by helicopter, makes a dry route to the source. Less sense of adventure, but access for many more – and blisters for those who wear wellingtons!

Once Afon Hafren (to give the river its Welsh name) has tumbled down its mountain, it fairly quickly takes on the characteristics of a river, not a stream. As it runs through a steep-sided valley, overhanging trees line the banks, preventing a view of the water from above; this proved to be an early example of a photographic problem encountered all the way to Gloucestershire which ruled out high, wide views of the snaking river in its pastoral setting.

From Newtown to just beyond Welshpool, the Montgomeryshire canal, today in various stages of restoration, runs a parallel course to Afon Hafren. In effect it acted as a proxy river here, enabling navigation and trade to reach Newtown and sustain its expansion before the railways came. At the same time it pre-empted any move to use the river itself.

Facing page: *'Severn breaks its neck' waterfall*

THE SOURCE

The river springs from the boggy summit ridge of Plynlimon. Previously the source was difficult to pinpoint amongst the many small marshy depressions, but today the new hard path laid by the Forestry Commission leads directly to it and beyond to Plynlimon's ridge. Stone slabs provide a dry route across the very wet mountain.

Afon Hafren very quickly asserts itself as a fast-flowing clear stream, running on a bed of pebbles under high peaty banks (see previous page to find out why a wellington boot should be there!).

HAFREN FOREST

After a relatively short run down the open mountain, the stream drops into the huge Hafren Forest, mostly through clearings which give it space and presence.

Blaen Hafren is a big waterfall, giving a good excuse for uphill walkers, who are by then more than halfway to the source, to pause and refresh themselves.

By the time it approaches the Forestry car park, Hafren has achieved a grander stature and progresses in an estate-like setting through the pines.

Below the forest the young river runs through a steep-sided valley carpeted with bracken and bluebells.

Converted chapels, as at Glynhafren (right), *are a feature of the high valley. At one of the first dwellings below the mountain, Joe Noble wades into Hafren, his own ad hoc back-garden swimming pool.*

LLANIDLOES

Llanidloes is the first town on the river. Its old industry is represented by a converted cloth mill (right) which would once have been driven by water power.

In summer the wide pebbly shallows where the Afon Clywedog joins Hafren become an annexe to the adjacent park.

PENSON'S BRIDGES

Dated 1846, Llandiman is the first of three iron bridges crossing Hafren built by Thomas Penson, county surveyor of Montgomery-shire. The other two are Brynderwen, Abermule, dated 1852 (page 24) and Caerhowel (right), two miles north-west of Montgomery, dated 1858 (plaque, below).

Penson also added an iron footway to the masonry bridge in Newtown (below right).

NEWTOWN

The river runs right through the centre of Newtown. Following repeated flooding, St Mary's church was abandoned in 1856; amongst the ruins, in a park by the river, stands a memorial to Robert Owen, early champion of workers' rights who was born in the town. The beautiful relief sculpture, showing Owen with an angel at his side and a range of craftsmen, was presented by the Co-operative Movement in 1902. Another memorial in the ruined church is to Sir Pryce Pryce-Jones, credited with pioneering the concept of mail order. His warehouse and factory still dominate the town centre – the last trace of Llanidloes' traditional industry of cloth weaving (see page 22).

Newtown's wealth was built on cloth mills; these flourished in conjunction with the terminus of the Montgomeryshire canal, which had its wharves at the east end of town in Llanllwchaiarn. The canal has been out of use for many decades and today there is nothing but the name plate 'Canal Street' and some large piles of rubble. 'Warehouse-style' apartments are rising. A mile to the west is an abandoned lock and the old canal bed, well defined as a broad grassy ditch beneath the may blossom (facing page).

Penarth weir (right)was built across the river to provide a permanent high-water level, with a leat feeding the canal.

The canal runs parallel with Afon Hafren between Newtown and Welshpool and is gradually being restored into working order, to re-connect with the main network into the Midlands and the Mersey. In the early nineteenth century its trade possibilities would negate any thoughts of making the river more navigable.

Abermule is the location of one of Penson's three iron bridges over Hafren (page 18), the casting of the outer ribs rather crudely proclaiming it to be Montgomery's second iron bridge (facing page).

Brynderwen Lock is on a restored section of the canal, but the dry sections to the east currently prevent through-traffic.

WELSHPOOL

Afon Hafren (henceforth the Severn!) avoids Welshpool, which instead celebrates its canal connections. Buttington Bridge to the north-east provides us with a first view of Breidden Hill, an emphatic background for many miles further.

2   THE UPPER NAVIGATION: POOL QUAY TO LEIGHTON

This chapter refers to navigation, but that has to be viewed as an historic fact only. Pool Quay just downstream from Welshpool was undoubtedly a commercial wharf, but it could never be used in the summer months when the river levels were low. In 1828 the Montgomeryshire canal was opened, with a lock and wharf a quarter of a mile away and direct connection to the canal systems of the Mersey and the Midlands; transport this high up the river became redundant, with Pool Quay, Royal Hill and other wharves above Shrewsbury falling into disuse.

Today the upper Severn has an air of faded importance about it, rather like an east-coast Victorian seaside town. One can only imagine the activity and sense of purpose it must once have enjoyed. Even in Shrewsbury itself, a sunny Saturday in June failed to produce any river activity during my visit, a state of affairs mitigated by the cub-scout canoeists seen at Welsh Bridge on another occasion *(facing page)*.

Photographing this largely empty riverscape was a lonely experience. Long walks to view the inaccessible banks built to prevent and contain floods, locally known as 'argys,' culminated more than once in detours round blocked routes and missing footbridges. There are some extreme meanders near Melverley, with the river coming back to within a few yards of itself after a mile; sadly, if there was a way of photographing the meanders and the argys from above, it eluded me.

Facing page: *Canoeing by Welsh Bridge, Shrewsbury*

POOL QUAY

Two miles east of Welshpool, Pool Quay was the upper limit for river navigation. When the Montgomeryshire canal opened in 1828, a lock and wharf linked it to the river by a still existing track – now meeting the river at an uninviting iron bridge. Today there is no sign of wharves or buildings on the tree-darkened river bank, though a mill and its associated pool of water remain just to the west. Other buildings at that site, now being converted to residential use, look more commercial than agricultural.

Facing page: Between the canal and the river stands the Powis Arms. Over the decades watermen have burnt a series of holes in an oak beam in the ceiling of the saloon, apparently with a hot poker. There are various legends attached: one is that the marks proved arriving with a cargo, but more probable is that the right to wield the poker was conferred by the purchase and consumption of a gallon of beer.

ROYAL HILL

Royal Hill, an almost unannounced country pub right by the river, is the only feature on the long country road between Melverley and Shrawardine. Once the river here was lined with wharves; today it is a popular family picnic spot, with a distant view of Rodney's Pillar on Breidden Hill (facing page).

At Crew Green the River Vyrnwy joins the Severn; the mud-caked nettles high on the bank (facing page) *bear witness to exceptional river levels in May 2006.*

The Severn meanders in tight loops across the wide flood plain beneath Breidden, which is laced with drainage ditches (including New Cut) and 'levées,' flood defence banks known locally as 'argys'. Up to two metres in height, they are hard to photograph but are here defined by the huge sluices set into the grassy bank (right). *Dry meadows on either side presumably offer the ability to flood farmland as a relief measure to prevent worse inundation downstream.*

Llandrinio Bridge (above), with its high semi-circular arches, is complete with flood markers (out of frame) reaching almost as high as the top of the centre arch.

Thomas Telford, the famous engineer who was county surveyor of Shropshire, rebuilt the bridge at Montford, his first since working as a mason's apprentice in his home town of Langholm. The date stone reads 1792.

The toll house (above right) came two decades later as part of his building of the Holyhead Road.

Telford's name will feature several times in this book. Montford makes an interesting comparison with Over (pages 96–7), a masonry bridge built by Telford some thirty-five years later.

Before and after Shrewsbury, the Severn takes a wildly meandering course and the town itself is contained in a large horseshoe bend. At the west side on the top of the bend is the Welsh Bridge: in the centre of the downstream balustrading (above) is an iron bar and pulley wheel (hidden by its top cover plate) to help pull barges over the shallows. On the east side is the English Bridge, with stone dolphins sitting proudly on the cutwaters (left).

A large part of the space within the bend is devoted to a park, the Quarry, which leads down to the river and Porthill footbridge (facing page). The townsfolk seem oblivious to the fabulous riverside setting: on a fine Saturday in June not a single boat was to be seen on this mile-long stretch of water.

On another visit at Welsh Bridge some of the town's cub-scouts were learning to canoe (page 28) – not the slick sculling of the School or Pengwern boat clubs, but at least a sign of another generation learning to enjoy the river.

Jack Mytton (left) *was a squire with more money than sense whose arrogant and usually drunken exploits are lodged in Shropshire legend. However, it has to be said that none of the traditional tales involves a mermaid!*

Atcham Bridge (facing page) *dates from 1770, so is a survivor of the great 1795 floods which destroyed many others.*

ATCHAM AND WROXETER

Atcham church is reputed to have used stone from the Roman site at Uriconium, near Wroxeter two miles away. Between the church and the bridge are deep pools which are well known to salmon fishermen. Could the camera have caught a fish jumping?

Wroxeter, just a stone's throw from the Severn, uses Roman columns for the gateway to its churchyard. Although the river is close, access is blocked: the track leading to an old ferry crossing (and beyond to the route of a Roman road on the opposite bank) is now a private drive.

THE WREKIN

Under the brooding dominance of the Wrekin, Vern Mark, who has fished at Cressage Bridge for sixty years was asked if he had caught anything that morning. 'Yes', he replied. 'Some worms.' Apparently his season hadn't started.

At Leighton (right) the Severn performs its final lazy meanders before taking on the serious task of breaking through Wenlock Edge.

3 ARTISANS AND NATURE: BUILDWAS TO BEWDLEY

At Buildwas the character of the Severn changes. Confronted with Wenlock Edge, the sluggish meandering river that has slowly wound its way across the flood plains since before Shrewsbury, now cuts its way into the Ironbridge Gorge. At the same time its former quietly pastoral surroundings give way to the busy built-up environment of Coalbrookdale, whose massive legacy of industrial history completely enmeshes and embraces the river too.

The building of the first iron bridge was a pivotal point in the progress of the Industrial Revolution. But the river itself played a big part. Even after the building of the canals, river transport, which had faded away above Shrewsbury, was thriving from Ironbridge downstream. As late as the 1850s the iron plates for Brunel's ss *Great Eastern*, which were forged at Coalbrookdale, were sent down the river on their way to London. By the early 1860s the Severn Valley Railway, running in direct competition with the river from Shrewsbury to Bewdley, caused terminal decline.

Could this have been prevented? No attempts had been made to make the river more navigable; a few weirs did keep summer water levels higher than otherwise, but the way round these obstacles were 'barge gutters,' cut channels containing shallow rapids allowing through only a limited amount of water. Teams of up to ten men 'bow-hauled' barges up these obstacles, and nowhere on these upper reaches were locks installed.

Conservatism ruled. At the end of the eighteenth century an attempt was made to use horses instead of manpower, but it was resisted by the teams of men. Ironically, today, two hundred years too late, a well argued lobby is in favour of locks and weirs to improve the navigation on these reaches so that pleasure boats can reach Shrewsbury.

The banks of the river through the gorge are inundated by history, which is well served by a collection of interrelated museums. The whole area is a World Heritage Site. Past Bridgnorth, the mood changes again, the valley broadening out into a restoration of its previous pastoral calm.

Facing page: *Severn Valley Railway at Victoria Bridge*

BUILDWAS

It is no coincidence that Buildwas Abbey was built adjacent to the Severn: the monks would have traded their wool by boat downstream. The floor of the chapter house (right) has tiles dating back to the middle ages.

The monks were a powerful force in the land and controlled the bridge. Just downstream is the modern power station (facing page) whose workforce use an old abbey building as a social club.

CORACLES

Facing page: *Mingling with the reflections of the power station (see page 49), Terry Kenny (right) demonstrates his coracle: he runs three courses a year in which enthusiasts build their own vessel (there must be quite a quantity hanging on Shropshire garage walls). A coracle race is held on August Bank Holiday.*

Coracles were once commonplace on the Severn. Built on a frame of ash slats (below right) with a skin of canvas coated with pitch, they were lightweight and easily portable and could be carried across the 'neck' of horshoe bends, cutting miles off a meandering river journey.

Facing page: *A family sets off downstream for Bridgnorth on a canoe camping expedition. The cast-iron Albert Edward Bridge dates from 1864, one of a pair with Victoria further downstream* (page 68).

Right: *Following restoration, the* Spry, *a boat designed for the lower reaches of the Severn, took river trips from Gloucester to Bristol and it is hoped she will soon be in the water again. The model* (far right), *of a smaller upper-river trow, is on display in Gloucester's Waterways Museum* (see page 100).

The first building by the river approaching Ironbridge is the old Coalbrookdale Company Warehouse (below), *built in high gothic style and now a museum. Between it and the water are the muddy remains of its old tracks used for loading trows and barges* (facing page). *The Wharfage is the street running along the river front to the Ironbridge; many of the buildings' warehouse origins are reflected in current usage.*

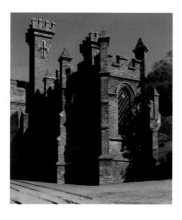

THE IRON BRIDGE

The opening of the Iron Bridge in 1781 flew a flag for the coming Industrial Revolution. Constructed from castings by Abraham Darby III in his Coalbrookdale furnaces, it is possible to argue that it was made to demonstrate the possibility as much as to fulfil a need. Later generations would refine the design of bridges and other structures; the Iron Bridge was built to some extent as if it were made of wood, with the spars joining the ribs utilising dovetail joints.

IRON BRIDGES

After the completion of the first iron bridge (viewed here from upstream on the Broseley bank), it was several years before other major bridges were built.

In 1799 the wooden bridge at Coalport was rebuilt with three cast-iron ribs, and again altered in 1818 to its present form (the original bridge being remembered in the name of the adjacent Woodbridge Hotel).

Right: *The modern asymmetric steel Broseley Bridge, south of Ironbridge, takes traffic from Darby's pedestrianised original and the weight-restricted Coalport Bridge.*

Iron in Ironbridge

Darby's Coalbrookdale furnace acts as a good memorial to the builder of the Iron Bridge. Casting a structure as large as a bridge was of course exceptional. Here, iron was a readily available local material and even everyday items could be made from it – like the kerb edges on the road (below) and the 'gravestones', which can be seen at the corrugated iron chapel in Blists Hill Museum (right), as well as in Benthall and Broseley graveyards. The broken anchor insignia (below right) was a mark of honour for watermen.

ABRAHAM·DARBY·1777

ABRAHAM·DARBY·1777

B E ♔ 1638 E ♔ B

COALPORT

Blists Hill Museum above Coalport contains the top end of the Hay Incline (facing page), a device for dropping boats down from the top section of the Shropshire canal to the bottom, on a level with the Severn.

Right: *The bottom section of the canal runs through the Coalport China Works, now a museum, but there was never a connection with the river (trans-shipments had to be unloaded across wharves).*

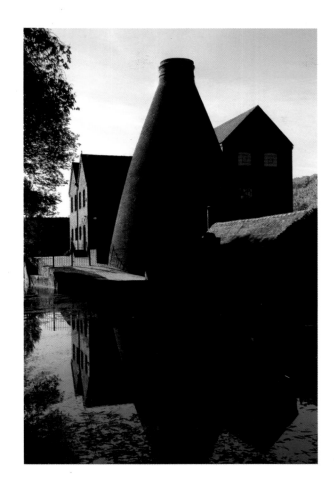

BRIDGNORTH

Facing page: *Bridgnorth's upper and lower towns are connected by the Castle Hill railway, cutting through the red sandstone with an incline of 1:1.5, said to be the steepest in Britain.*

Right: *The Severn bridge is another by Thomas Telford.*

There are almost no ferries left running across the Severn; Hampton Lode (facing page) *claims to be the last. It is unique in that it is driven by the power of the current. To stop the ferry drifting downstream it is connected by a pulley wheel to a wire slung across the river* (far right).

Below right: *Just below the ferry, the wide shallow rapids mark the site of a ford.*

The importance the river had for trade is emphasised by towpath bridges at the outflow of Borle Brook (above right) *and Mor Brook. In 1772 the towpath from Bewdley to Coalbrookdale was made a turnpike trust: the bridges were built in the early part of the nineteenth century as part of the improvement to the path, so that horses could take over from the teams of men who traditionally pulled the barges.*

UPPER ARLEY

Facing page: *At Upper Arley the ferry has been replaced by a footbridge, but the charming stone-built quay remains.*

Right: *A mile downstream, the Severn Valley Railway crosses the river on the 1861 cast-iron Victoria Bridge.*

Facing page: *Beyond the balustrading of Telford's Bewdley Bridge, rows of merchant's houses line the river quay. Looking back from downstream, a fisherman* (right) *works the shallows below.*

The rowing club, above, *with boats out training, have their home on the Wribbenhall wharf, where Bewdley's best-known family of rivermen, the Beales, traded with their trows.*

4   THE LOWER NAVIGATION: STOURPORT TO OVER BRIDGE

Boating at last: the lower navigation can be accepted as a present-day reality. The stretch of river from Stourbridge to Gloucester is managed by British Waterways and is tamed by five locks and weirs – the first at Lincomb, just below Stourport, under whose red-rock cliffs the picture opposite was taken. As Stourport connects with the canal system, the river is busy with pleasure boats, many modelled on traditional narrowboats.

Stourport did not exist until the late eighteenth century when James Brindley, the 'father' of the English canals, made it the Severn junction for the Staffordshire and Worcestershire canal. Brindley's vision was a network of canals which would link up with and depend on, not replace, the four great rivers – Trent, Mersey, Severn and Thames. Stourport was a pivotal point on this system. Its wharves and warehouses serviced the trade as river trows from Bristol and Gloucester transferred their cargoes to canal narrowboats bound for the Midlands. Today Stourport thrives as a canal marina and is the upper limit of navigation on the river.

Worcester had a similar set of docks in its southern suburb of Diglis, where the Birmingham canal met the Severn. At Tewkesbury and Upton, well-stocked marinas would not look out of place on the Norfolk Broads. Now the old rivermen's pubs have a *raison d'être* beyond being motorists' destinations for Sunday lunch: many have newly restored wharves which are well used by the river traffic.

Thomas Telford built four major road bridges across the Severn in this section, three of which were single-span cast iron. Haw has been replaced and Holt Fleet strengthened with concrete, but Mythe remains true to the original. Just to the north of Gloucester, Over Bridge, with its elegant stonework and daringly flat arch, is a fine reminder that before becoming the master of the sructural use of iron, Telford had trained as a mason and had ambitions to be an architect.

Facing page: *Downstream from Lincomb Lock*

A dockside crane and original warehouse survive in Stourport's docks on the Staffordshire and Worcestershire Canal. A series of locks connect the canal wharves to the Severn.

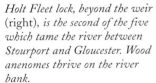

Holt Fleet lock, beyond the weir (right), *is the second of the five which tame the river between Stourport and Gloucester. Wood anenomes thrive on the river bank.*

Facing page: *A pleasure boat passes under Holt Fleet Bridge, built by Telford but heavily reinforced with latterday concrete.*

WORCESTER

Worcester Cathedral stands timeless on the river bank; a short distance downstream, flood markers (facing page) decorate the walls of Watergate, from which Wayne Gibbons (right) runs a ferry to the meadow opposite.

DIGLIS

Diglis, on the south side of Worcester, is where the Birmingham and Worcester canal meets the river, through a pair of locks. As at Stourport there were extensive inland docks, most of which are at present being re-developed for housing. The Top Basin provides residential mooring.

Edmund Richards (right) lives in Diglis Terrace, standing just beyond the towpath and some four or five feet above it – not high enough to prevent all the houses being flooded in the year 2000. 'Some of my neighbours got big insurance payouts,' says Edmund. 'I didn't bother to claim – just waited for it to drain off and then cleaned up.' He has now sold his house to live closer to his son.

UPTON ON SEVERN

Upton (sometimes referred to as 'Teashop-on-Severn') is a pretty town, once host to river wharves. Its modern bridge (right) *provides a distant view of the Malvern Hills.*

    Below: *Just downstream, near Ryall, a rare commercial use is found for the river as barges unload at a sand and gravel depot.*

TEWKESBURY APPROACHES

Upstream from Tewkesbury, Mythe Bridge (facing page) *offers a chance to see one of Telford's finest iron bridges (built to the same pattern as the celebrated Craigellachie over the Spey).*

Tewkesbury's mills and wharves are in fact on the Avon, which joins the Severn across the meadow named Severn Ham.

UPPER LODE

Approaching Upper Lode Lock, Tewkesbury Abbey comes into view across Severn Ham (right).

The lock itself is a most unusual design. The river below Tewkesbury is relatively shallow but still slightly tidal: the bulbous basin within the lock was designed to hold several boats until high water could give them a safer passage downstream.

Today best known as the location of the Boat Inn, Ashleworth is the site of an old wharf and ferry.

Above: *Just downstream, the importance of the levée as a flood defence is shown by the heavy-duty gateway cut into it for a boat-launching ramp.*

ASHLEWORTH BARN

This celebrated tithe barn is strategically placed some fifty yards from the Ashleworth Quay. The flood marker in the fore-ground tells its own tale.

A short distance upstream from Maisemore the river divides, creating the two-mile-long Alney Island, before rejoining below Gloucester. The old lock and weir at Maisemore are now abandoned, the weir here defined by high water in spate across it.

Facing page: From the eastern channel the tower of Gloucester cathedral signals the approach to the city, seen across flooded meadows in the year 2000.

MAISEMORE

At the Maisemore wharf of
J. Young and Son, Douglas and
Philip Young, the grandson and
great-grandson of the founder of
the firm, still trade coal, though
deliveries are no longer by river.

OVER BRIDGE *(page 96)*

Before the river re-unites (page
92), the western (Maisemore)
channel passes under Over Bridge,
historically the lowest bridge on
the Severn. Telford would have
used iron here, but the town
worthies who were his clients
insisted on a 'real bridge' of stone.
The result is one of the great
engineer's masterpieces. The
chamfered cutaway of the arch is
said to facilitate the passage of

flood water, but in fact the worst
floods never reach this height:
certainly it adds visual lightness to
the design, further increasing the
'flatness' of the already low-slung
curve. This was Telford's last
substantial masonry bridge and its
elegance and daring can be
compared with the solid
workmanlike job at Montford,
built thirty-five years earlier
(page 36).

5 THE TIDEWAY: GLOUCESTER TO SEVERN BEACH

Just as the Severn seems to be realising its potential as an important navigable river, it loses it again. As in the upper reaches, the river below Gloucester has been neutered by a canal and – to add insult to injury – blocked by a weir. The only way to progress downstream (unless you are in a coracle!) is to enter Gloucester Docks which lead to the ship canal which bypasses the river to join it again at Sharpness.

The Sharpness canal, opened in 1828, boosted the prosperity of Gloucester Docks and made enormous sense as the stretch of river it avoids is fiercely tidal and very shallow over shifting sandbanks. However, unlike the upper river, the reaches between Sharpness and Gloucester have retained a vitality of their own. Even though they are in effect on a dead-end, the old Forest of Dean docks at Lydney and Bullo are still busy in their different ways.

Fishing has always been an important aspect of life on the Gloucestershire Severn; there are fewer salmon in the river and fewer men attempting to catch them, but the traditions linger on. Fishing for elvers (baby eels) is a strong tradition on the upper tidal reaches of the river: licenced or illicit, it is extremely lucrative, (an export market even exists in Japan) and although the elver-fishing season is short, there many tales of riverside squabbles over territory and catches. Although I did my best to follow up contacts, I was never able to clinch a photographic outing and was told that to venture onto the night-time riverbank as an unknown would be as foolhardy as looking for moonshiners brewing whisky in the Mississippi backwoods.

Where does the Severn become the Bristol Channel? The river has been two miles wide before it narrows at the Severn Bridge near Chepstow, to widen again at the Second Crossing. At Severn Beach the riverbank feels more like the seaside, and my story ends as the mountain water from Wales blends in with the salty Atlantic.

Facing page: *Second Crossing from Severn Beach*

GLOUCESTER HERITAGE

Set in the heart of Gloucester, a lock from the eastern channel of the Severn leads up to the docks, where the water level is higher than the river. The view to the cathedral is across the lock gates of a thriving dry-dock boat business.

Facing page: Situated in an old warehouse, the Waterways Museum exhibits include the old barges moored on the adjacent wharves.

GLOUCESTER DOCKS

The importance Gloucester Docks had as a trading port is underlined by the survival of its ranks of Victorian warehouses.

At the southern end, the dock leads directly, via the Llanthony lift bridge, into the Sharpness canal. Opened in 1827 this ship canal provided a safe route past the most dangerous section of the tidal Severn, where shallow water and shifting sands imposed a severe limit on boats able to reach Gloucester. The canal opening led to a huge expansion in the city's trade, but almost completely put an end to traffic on the bypassed river (page 99).

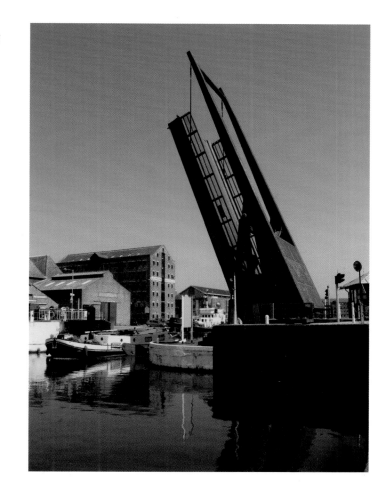

SHARPNESS DOCK

*Some ten miles downstream,
the canal rejoins the river through
Sharpness Dock, which still trades
in dry goods, grain and cement.
However, traffic entering the docks
for the canal is rarely commercial –
this flotilla of white cruisers is
bound for the marina at Upton
after an excursion to Bristol.*

ON THE LEVÉE

As on the Welsh border, flood prevention banks (known locally as 'cribs') follow the river along this tidal section. Here we see cows grazing on the crib at Minsterworth, and cowslips in bloom at Broad Oak.

THE BORE

The heavy tides in the Bristol
Channel combined with the
distorted funnel shape of the
Severn give rise to the unusual
phenomenon of the 'bore' – a wave
moving up the river at the head of
the incoming tide, sometimes as
much as two metres high. Anyone
who has tried to help children dam
a tiny stream knows the force of
moving water. To see a wave of
water surging up the wide river
and sending its flow into reverse is
awe-inspiring, and large crowds
line the banks when a 'big bore' is
predicted.

   Even unannounced
miniatures have their devotees.
The bore begins at Newnham;
just beyond, at Broad Oak, surfers
launch themselves onto the wave
in an elemental tussle to harness
its power (on a big bore they can
ride miles upriver). Jet-skiers (just
excluded from my picture) impose
their own brand of noisy fun,
throwing up plumes of spray as
they jump the bore and corner in
its choppy wake.

Historically, Forest of Dean trade was carried on at wharves at Newnham and Broad Oak and in Lydney's muddy creek (known locally as a 'pill'). Huge increases in coal output in the early nineteenth century led to a dock being built at tiny Bullo Pill, followed by a tidal lock and harbour at Lydney (facing page).

Today Bullo is host to ship demolition and 'recycling,' while Lydney, the subject of major refurbishment as a 'heritage site,' is often visited by historic ships.

At low tide on a sandbank near Gatcombe, a lone salmon fisherman uses a traditional 'lave' net – rather like a child fishing for minnows, except that this triangular net has three-foot-long sides.

By the river at Broad Oak, Eric Jack makes 'putcher' baskets with hazel from the Somerset Levels.

FISHING AT AWRE

Facing page: *The Cadogan family set out their rank of 'putcher' traps at Awre at the beginning of the salmon-fishing season. The traps face upstream, which seems paradoxical as the fish they aim to catch are heading up the river to spawn; as the tide turns to ebb back downstream, the salmon 'rest,' going with the water, and become trapped in the funnel-shaped baskets.*

Right: *Chris Cadogan shows off a fine catch.*

PURTON AND PURTON

*At a point where the river, which
has been a mile wide, narrows
again towards Sharpness, it is
surprising to find a community
named Purton on both sides of the
river. In 1874 the river was
bridged at this point by a railway
linking Brunel's South Wales line
on the west side to his Gloucester
and Bristol line on the east. The
bridge was demolished in 1960
following an incident in which
two petrol tankers exploded after
colliding with a pier in the fog.*

*The remaining column was
the central pier of a swing bridge
carrying the railway over the
Sharpness Canal.*

TOWERS ON THE EAST SIDE

The viewing tower of Slimbridge Wildfowl Centre rises over its low marshy site between the canal and the river above Sharpness.

From Lydney Dock, the blue-and-white reactor buildings of the nuclear power station at Oldbury five miles away can be seen towering over the sandy riverbed at low tide.

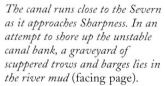

The canal runs close to the Severn as it approaches Sharpness. In an attempt to shore up the unstable canal bank, a graveyard of scuppered trows and barges lies in the river mud (facing page).

Above *and* right: *From sites at Beachley and Sharpness, the Severn Area Rescue Association (SARA) runs an inshore search and rescue service. Navigation markers and lights define the dangerous channel below Sharpness.*

SEVERN BRIDGE

Facing page: *The Severn Road Bridge rises magnificently over the old car-ferry jetty at Beachley, near Chepstow.*

   Right: *Across the river on the Bristol side, the boards and piling of the terminal at Old Passage rot gently into the marshy foreshore.*

SECOND CROSSING *(page 124)*

Built some three miles downstream to relieve the traffic volumes on the original bridge, the 'Second Crossing' is seen from the old jetty of the New Passage ferry.

INDEX

Facing page: *The Severn from May Hill*

ACKNOWLEDGEMENTS

Many thanks to all those who agreed to appear in this book, and to:

Karl Hooton
Darren Larkham
Paul Manning
John Powell (Ironbridge)
John Powell (Broad Oak)
Jim Ralph
Barrie Trinder
Peter Wallace

The following photos were first used in a previous book:

Page 36, Montford Toll House: *On Tour with Thomas Telford* (2004)
Page 108, Severn Bore: *A Portrait of Dean* (2003)
Page 110, Severn Railway Bridge: *Work in the Woods* (2002)